IMAGES
of America

CAMP RIPLEY
1930–1960

IMAGES
of America

CAMP RIPLEY
1930–1960

Sandra Alcott Erickson

ARCADIA
PUBLISHING

Published by Arcadia Publishing
Charleston SC, Chicago IL, Portsmouth NH, San Francisco CA

Printed in the United States of America

Library of Congress Catalog Card Number: 2007924798

For all general information contact Arcadia Publishing at:
Telephone 843-853-2070
Fax 843-853-0044
E-mail sales@arcadiapublishing.com
For customer service and orders:
Toll-Free 1-888-313-2665

Visit us on the Internet at www.arcadiapublishing.com

Maj. Gen. Ellard A. Walsh became Minnesota's adjutant general beginning in October 1925, when he was appointed as acting adjutant general. He served in this position until his retirement on October 2, 1949. It was under his guidance and through his extraordinary vision for the future that Camp Ripley became a reality. He also served as president of the National Guard Association of the United States from 1927 to 1928 and 1943 to 1957. In his memory, Camp Ripley was formally dedicated as the General E. A. Walsh Training Center on September 9, 1984.

CONTENTS

ACKNOWLEDGMENTS

Special thanks go to Sgt. 1st Class (Ret.) James L. Erickson; board of directors and staff of the Minnesota Military Museum; Leland Smith, archivist of the Minnesota Military Museum; Minnesota State adjutant general Maj. Gen. Larry Shellito; Minnesota Department of Military Affairs; Col. Richard Weaver, post commander of Camp Ripley; the Facilities Maintenance Office at Camp Ripley; Sylvia Stoner; and the Morrison County Historical Society.

INTRODUCTION

Camp Ripley is the successor to Minnesota's first permanent National Guard training facility, Camp Lakeview, which was located in southern Minnesota near Lake Pepin and the town of Lake City. The lands that comprised Camp Lakeview were leased from the town of Lake City by the State of Minnesota beginning in 1891 under the terms of a 40-year lease.

Following World War I, due to changes in tactics and weapons the size of Camp Lakeview was recognized to be inadequate, so Adj. Gen. Ellard A. Walsh searched for land upon which to build a new facility that would better meet the requirements of modern military training. After reviewing many potential sites, a tract of approximately 12,000 acres north of the town of Little Falls was selected and submitted to the Department of War for approval. In late 1929, the site was approved, and the lands were purchased by the State of Minnesota. Surveying began immediately; plans were completed and sent to the National Guard bureau and the quartermaster general in Washington, D.C., for review. The approval was ultimately received, but not until late April 1930. The requested federal funds for construction of the new facility were available only until June 30 of that year, which meant that all the contracts for construction would have to be executed on or before that date. Any funds not obligated for the construction project by June 30 would have to be returned to the federal government. The bidding process began immediately after receipt of the approval from Washington. Construction contracts were awarded in early June, and construction began on June 5, 1930.

While federal funds would pay for most of the buildings and infrastructure in the first phase of construction, the State of Minnesota also provided funds for part of the project. Since the Mississippi River stood between the new facility and the branch railroad line that would play a key role in transporting troops and equipment to Camp Ripley, a bridge was needed that would accommodate railroad and automobile use. The state took bids on a contract to build a 410-foot bridge across the river that included a railroad track in the bridge deck. Contracts were also awarded by the state for the building of the spur track that would connect the camp with the branch railroad line on the east side of the Mississippi River and for construction of the highway leading from the existing road on the east side of the river and into the new training camp. The construction of the five-trunk telephone system was also built with funds from the State of Minnesota.

The first phase of Camp Ripley's construction consisted of one regimental training area with separate areas for officers and enlisted men. An additional regimental compound—identical to the first—was constructed beginning in April 1931, and it was scheduled to be completed by June 1, 1931, in time to accommodate troops for summer training.

In December 1930, the new facility was officially named Camp Ripley after Fort Ripley, a frontier fort in the area that had been closed and abandoned by the federal government in 1877. It is a little-known fact that the initial land purchases for the establishment of Camp Ripley did not include the ruins of Fort Ripley. The fort site and ruins were acquired later by the State of Minnesota and subsequently incorporated into the Camp Ripley military reservation.

Troops were housed in tents from the opening of Camp Ripley in 1931 until the late 1950s. Tents were usable only for the summer season and proved too costly to maintain due to deterioration from exposure to the elements. With an eye toward the future and the hope that Camp Ripley's usefulness would expand beyond just summer use, the tents were replaced with small metal buildings called hutments, which are still in place today.

There are several buildings on Camp Ripley that have historical significance. One example of this is Valhalla, the governor's lodge. It serves as the home for the governor when he visits Camp Ripley. Valhalla is a beautiful log building constructed of lodge pole pine by the Civilian Conservation Corps (CCC) in 1937. Former president Harry S. Truman stayed at Valhalla twice, and Sen. Eugene McCarthy was another of its distinguished guests. In addition to providing lodging for the governor, today Valhalla is also used for VIP visits, lodging, and social events.

One of the camp's most recognizable features—a 3,400-foot-long black granite wall that incorporates the main gate as well as the east and west gates—was meticulously constructed of locally quarried granite by Works Progress Administration (WPA) workers. It took eight years to complete.

The Ray S. Miller Airfield was built in 1933. Maj. Ray Miller is credited with the creation of the 109th Observation Squadron, which was the predecessor to the Minnesota Air National Guard and the first federally recognized National Guard air unit in the United States.

Camp Ripley has several sites of archaeological interest within its borders. There are several cemeteries and individual grave sites there, most of which were associated with frontier homesteads and abandoned churches. Tribes of native Dakota and Chippewa Indians lived in the area prior to 1858 when Minnesota became a state. Some archaeological studies have been completed, and there are some mounds that are speculated to be Native American burial mounds.

Another little-known fact is that Camp Ripley was federalized, or leased for use by the federal government and removed from state control, during World War II. The facility was used for the training of airbase security personnel and military police. The 173rd Station Hospital was also operated there during 1943. However, because Camp Ripley was only a summer training facility prior to federalization, it proved impractical to use the facility during the winter months, so the lease was ultimately not renewed by the federal government and the camp returned to state control in the fall of 1943.

Following the end of World War II, Minnesota National Guard troops who had served as part the 34th Infantry Division were mustered out of federal service. This prompted a reorganization of the entire National Guard. The 34th Infantry Division was moved to Iowa, and the 47th Infantry Division was created to take its place. An intensive recruiting program took place in order to raise the strength of the National Guard to federal requirements, and the first summer training encampment at Camp Ripley following World War II took place in 1947. The 47th Infantry Division was federalized in January 1951 for service in the Korean War, and the troops were sent to Camp Rucker in Alabama for training.

Also in 1951, the Minnesota state legislature appropriated $700,000 for the purchase of land to expand Camp Ripley. The size of the camp was expanded to 45,000 acres at that time, and since then, additional land purchases have increased the size of the facility to approximately 53,000 acres. It is one of the largest National Guard training facilities in the United States.

One

BEFORE CAMP RIPLEY

Arrival of First Regt. Inf. Minnesota National Guard at Camp "Lakeview" Lake City, Minn. June 12, 1911.

While the Minnesota National Guard began holding regular summer training encampments in the early 1880s in various locations around the state, Camp Lakeview was the first permanent training camp. It was located in a scenic site on the shores of Lake Pepin, which is actually an exceptionally wide area in the Mississippi River south of the town of Lake City in southern Minnesota. The acreage that comprised Camp Lakeview was leased to the Minnesota National Guard for use as a military training facility on a 40-year lease beginning in 1891. However, following World War I it became evident that the facility was too small due to changes in weaponry, battle tactics, and federal government requirements, so Adj. Gen. Ellard A. Walsh began seeking a site for a new training camp beginning in 1925.

Each summer, most soldiers arriving at Camp Lakeview did so by train. Troops slept in tents. The only permanent structures on the site were an infirmary, pictured here, manned by medical units that used a horse-drawn ambulance; a mess hall; and a building that served as both headquarters and warehouse. Training consisted of marksmanship, horsemanship, and discipline, as well as drill and ceremony. Evenings were spent socializing and relaxing.

While soldiers training at Camp Lakeview slept in tents, a mess hall was one of the three permanent wooden buildings constructed on the site. This photograph shows men waiting in line for chow with mess kits in hand.

DRESS PARADE - CAMP LAKEVIEW, MINN.
LAKE CITY, MINN

Each weeklong encampment was usually highlighted with a parade and a picnic for the families and friends of the soldiers. One year, however, this pleasant activity ended in tragedy when the river steamer *Sea Wing*, which was transporting the visitors back home in the evening, capsized in a sudden storm. Ninety-eight people lost their lives, and soldiers from Camp Lakeview spent days rescuing survivors and recovering the bodies of the dead.

Camp Ripley was named after a U.S. frontier fort in the area known as Fort Ripley. This watercolor painting depicting Fort Ripley, entitled *Old Fort Ripley 1864*, was painted by Paul Kramer of St. Paul in 1991. It offers a perspective of the fort from the opposite side of the Mississippi River. Part of the land set aside as the Fort Ripley military reserve was actually located on the opposite side of the river from the fort. That tract of nearly 58,000 acres was originally set aside for agricultural use to produce food for the fort's occupants and to provide a source of wood. However, military occupation of the land also prevented settlers from inhabiting the area immediately adjacent to the fort. In the foreground is the Red River Oxcart Trail that connected St. Paul and Winnipeg. The original painting is on exhibit at the Minnesota Military Museum.

Heeding lessons learned from the history of other frontier forts in the area that were built without stockades, Fort Ripley was enclosed by a stockade that surrounded its clapboard buildings and stone ammunition storage hut. All timber was also cleared from the area immediately surrounding the stockade to allow for better visibility. Additionally, the construction of Fort Ripley's stockade incorporated three blockhouses. The fort was garrisoned by U.S. Army troops from the spring of 1849 through June 1861, when the army troops were withdrawn from the fort and sent to fight in the Civil War. From that time until the end of the Civil War in 1865, the fort was garrisoned by regiments of Minnesota volunteer infantry.

OLD POWDER HOUSE OF FORT RIPLEY, MINN.

The last troops left Fort Ripley in 1877. In 1879, a prairie fire destroyed a large portion of the fort's wooden buildings and stockade. The remaining buildings were dismantled by area settlers. In 1880, the lands comprising the military reserve were turned over to the Department of the Interior for sale to settlers. The stone powder house, pictured here, was the only building that remained of the old fort. The foundation of this stone structure is still visible today, but Camp Ripley has placed signs on the old fort site marking where the original buildings stood.

Two

THE NEW TRAINING CAMP

Construction of Camp Ripley began in 1930. During World War I, the U.S. military had constructed its facilities almost entirely of wood, which deteriorated badly after maintenance funds were cut by Congress following the end of the war. In the late 1920s, a new building program was instituted by Congress to rebuild troop housing facilities. With an eye toward cost effectiveness and durability, under the guidance of the U.S. Army Quartermaster Corps buildings on Camp Ripley were largely constructed of concrete block.

What is now known as Minnesota Highway 371 was, at the time Camp Ripley was constructed, State Trunk Highway 27. In 1930, Highway 27 was paved with concrete all the way from the Iowa border to the town of Brainerd approximately 25 miles to the north of the Camp Ripley site. It was the main road to Minneapolis and St. Paul. Running parallel to Highway 27 was the main line of the Northern Pacific Railroad. A spur track was constructed from this line to the west over the new bridge that crossed the Mississippi River. It entered Camp Ripley through what is now known as the east gate.

When searching for a site for the new training camp, Adj. Gen. Ellard A. Walsh used the recommendations of his predecessor, Adj. Gen. W. F. Rhinow, as a guideline for determining which sites deserved further consideration. Accessibility to the railroad and to a major roadway was important for rapid mobilization of troops. The site ultimately approved by the Department of War in 1929 met these requirements, as long as a bridge to allow both automobile and railroad traffic could be constructed across the Mississippi River. The building of a bridge across a major river required formal congressional approval. A special act of Congress provided that approval in February 1930. The State of Minnesota paid for construction of the new, 410-foot bridge that incorporated a railroad track in the bridge deck. The bridge is the only one of its type in Minnesota.

Camp Ripley's most recognizable features are its black granite main gate and perimeter walls. The Works Progress Administration (WPA) began building the structures in 1935 and completed them in 1942. The wall itself is three feet high, two feet deep, and is constructed of dry-laid black granite. The granite used was waste stone procured from the abandoned Freedhem granite quarry. There are two additional entrance gates east of the main gate, one of which is near the post commander's residence. The main gate itself consists of two 40-foot pylons of mortared, black granite. Inside these pylons are two 16-foot rectangular gateposts also of mortared, black granite. There are pedestrian entrances on either side of the 40-foot pylons. Architect Philip Bettenburg designed the main gate to resemble the U.S. Army engineering crest.

The building that later became known as Nelson Hall was Camp Ripley's first post headquarters. Construction was completed in November 1930, at a total cost of $12,461.30. It addition to offices, it contained an officers' lounge, kitchen, and mess hall that would accommodate about 50 officers. Officers billets, or sleeping quarters, were located on the second floor. Civilian cooks were employed to make the meals. Civilians were also hired as housekeepers and waitresses.

Administration Bldg. Camp Ripley, Minn - 16

Rossberg Hall, also known as Building U-1, was built in 1931. At that time, it was known as the arsenal. Funding for construction of Rossberg Hall was provided by the State of Minnesota. While most of the buildings on Camp Ripley were of simple, concrete block construction, Rossberg Hall was one of the few that had a brick veneer. Architectural flourishes were extremely limited due to the need to conform to federally approved building plans, but the design of Rossberg Hall incorporates some art deco characteristics. The railroad tracks coming into Camp Ripley pass on the south side of Rossberg Hall, and this area was routinely used for troops to enter and exit the trains, as shown in the photograph below.

ARMORY — CAMP RIPLEY, MINNESOTA 203

Camp Ripley's armory was one of the approximately 90 buildings constructed by individuals employed under the federal New Deal program. It is a concrete block building with brick veneer. Like nearby Rossberg Hall, the armory had some art deco architectural details. Construction was completed in 1937, and total cost of the building was $169,769.66. The central feature of the interior of the armory was a large, open area called the drill floor where formations were held. The original construction also housed a stage, but after a fire the area was reconstructed and the stage was eliminated. Prior to 1953 when the new camp theater and visual aids training facility was built, the armory served as the main post theater.

The first hospital to be constructed on Camp Ripley in 1932 consisted of a wood frame covered by canvas. Like the tents that housed the troops during the summer annual training periods, the canvas was removed and stored for the winter in an effort to preserve it. The hospital was operated by National Guard medical units.

Camp Ripley's first permanent hospital was built in 1938 as part of the ongoing WPA building program. The total cost of construction was $4,856.56, with $1,400 of the funding coming from the State of Minnesota and the remainder from the federal government. It was located on the far south end of area one and was the next building east of the service club. In 1953, a house was built in between the service club and the hospital that served as nurses' quarters.

Camp Ripley had its own nursery where approximately 35 different species of plants were raised. The nurserymen tended approximately 11,000 plants. At one time, the nursery was seeded with over 75,000 evergreens. The Civilian Conservation Corps (CCC) planted 200,000 evergreens on Camp Ripley and did extensive general conservation work during approximately a one-and-a-half-year period. The aerial photograph below shows the location of the camp nursery to the northwest of the main gate.

The earliest sections of Camp Ripley's black granite wall were constructed in 1934 and 1935 with funding provided by Federal Emergency Relief Administration (FERA). Only a chain-link fence along the highway existed prior to the wall's construction, and it is believed the project could have been intended as highway and roadside beautification. Plans for the two 1,200-foot black granite walls on either side of the east approach to the newly constructed bridge across the Mississippi River were prepared as a joint venture by the Minnesota National Guard and the State of Minnesota Department of Highways in 1934. Actual construction of the wall and its turrets was completed by the WPA. Note the railroad depot with a sign entitled, "Camp Ripley Junction" in the background.

THE LONE SENTINAL
ENTRANCE TO CAMP RIPLEY.

14

In 1934 and 1935, as part of the FERA highway beautification project, which included construction of the first two sections of the granite wall, a raised terrace was constructed between the two forks of the road leading from Highway 27 toward the Mississippi River bridge. The words *Camp Ripley* were placed in stone into the sloped sides of the terrace. Placed on the top was an artillery field gun, which came to be known as the "Lone Sentinel." In later years, the field gun was replaced by a tank.

THE LONE SENTINEL CAMP RIPLEY

Camp Ripley's custodian lived on site when the camp first opened, and the first house to be constructed on Camp Ripley was the custodian's residence. It was completed in 1931 at a total cost of $6,549.50. Since the house was located near the main entrance to the camp, its general appearance was important, so the plans specified a brick veneer for a more formal and esthetically pleasing look. Architecturally, the home is a modified English cottage style.

The first enlisted men's BOQ (bachelor officers' quarters) house was built in 1939. Two more were built in 1941 by the WPA at a cost of $12,106. The State of Minnesota funded $250 of that amount. These houses were located immediately south of the custodian's house.

While Camp Ripley first opened in 1931, the post commander, Col. Raymond A. Rossberg, and his wife, Bonnie, lived in a rented house in Little Falls. It was not until 1941 that the camp commander's house was built. The total cost for the structure was $30,322. Bonnie was very instrumental in reviewing plans for the house and suggesting modifications that would make the house more functional, not only for themselves but for future occupants. Prior to her marriage, she had been employed as an interior decorator. One of the changes she suggested was the expansion of the planned single garage to a double one. At her suggestion, closet space in the house was expanded, and plans were changed for the central stairwell, which made it one of the most memorable features of the house.

A typical infantry regimental area at Camp Ripley consisted of separate sections for officers and enlisted men. In the front were the regimental staff officers' tents in between the regimental headquarters building on the left and the officers' mess on the right. The regimental headquarters contained offices and the officers' club. There were two officers' bathhouses and latrines in each area. The company officers' tents were located behind the regimental officers' area. Ten enlisted men's mess halls were next, and behind them were the enlisted men's tents. Behind the tents were the enlisted men's latrines and the vehicle parking area or motor pool.

The first housing for troops—both officers and enlisted men—on Camp Ripley was canvas tents. The tent canvas was placed over a wood frame. The canvas was removed and stored inside for the winter in order to minimize damage from exposure to the elements. Despite these efforts, however, the canvas proved to be very expensive and tedious to maintain. In the late 1950s, the tents were replaced by metal buildings called hutments.

The tents were located on raised platforms, as pictured in the photograph above. By the end of 1932, a total of 321 tent platforms had been built.

In anticipation that Camp Ripley could potentially become a mobilization site or a regular army training center during World War II, six two-story, wood frame barracks were built at the north end of the airfield in anticipation of increased need for troop housing. These barracks were constructed based on standardized plans from the U.S. Army Quartermaster Corps. Beginning in July 1942, the Department of War leased Camp Ripley for use in training army aviation and infantry units; however, long-term use of the facility by the federal government was not to be. An unexpected and very unusual snowstorm in September 1942 caused the Department of War to change its plans because the camp's facilities were largely designed for summer use only. Camp Ripley was returned to state control in the summer of 1943.

Each infantry regimental area contained both officers' and enlisted men's latrines. In the officers' area there were two latrines that served also as bathhouses. In the enlisted men's area there were four of these buildings capable of accommodating 250 men each. As with the other buildings, U.S. Army Quartermaster Corps design specifications were followed and the latrines were constructed of concrete block with gabled roofs. Each latrine contained showerheads and lavatory facilities as well as closets. A laundry room, complete with tubs and washboards, was housed in each latrine. The first latrines were completed in 1930.

Each regimental area contained mess halls with attached kitchens for cooking food and feeding the officers and troops. In the enlisted men's area, there were 15 mess halls with attached kitchens, one for each unit of over 50 men. Each enlisted men's mess hall accommodated 80 to 100 men at a time and contained an orderly room and a supply room.

This is an example of an officer's mess hall. Kitchens were equipped with permanent ranges, sinks, screened wet and dry garbage racks, vegetable racks, a pantry, and a 50-cubic-foot electric refrigerator. Also contained in each mess hall was a hose-and-reel firefighting system capable of handling any fires in the immediate vicinity.

Some combination mess halls were built on Camp Ripley. These were designed to be used by both enlisted men and officers.

The first two phases of construction at Camp Ripley during 1930 and 1931 began the rapid development of the post's utility area, which was located immediately south of the airfield. The first steel water storage tank, capable of holding 100,000 gallons, was built in 1930. The above photograph was taken when it was still incomplete. Below is a 1934 aerial photograph of the utility area. It shows the progress of construction of both the infantry regimental areas (on the east side of the airfield) and the utility area.

Two 100-foot wells were drilled in the utility area in 1930, and two 165-foot wells were drilled in 1931. In order to meet the growing post's demand for water, an additional well was drilled in 1937 by the McCarthy Well Company. This photograph memorializes the event. The next deep well was drilled in 1949.

Pictured here, the facility for the treatment of drinking water was built by the WPA in 1937.

There was one warehouse building constructed in each infantry regimental area on Camp Ripley. The above building is an example of a regimental warehouse. In addition, the area south of the airfield, known in Camp Ripley's early days as the utility area, was also set aside for construction of additional warehouses as part of the camp infrastructure and expansion plans for the future.

Warehouses of various sizes were constructed throughout the utility area. Some were used for storage of goods and military vehicles, while others were used as maintenance garages. This photograph shows an example of a maintenance garage.

The custodian's office, pictured here, was located in one of the warehouses in the camp utility area.

Beginning in 1941, larger warehouses were also constructed that were designated as 50-truck warehouses.

The camp commissary was a 40-foot-by-200-foot concrete building with a full basement. It was the central distribution point for food for the camp mess halls and contained an office, issue counter, and three refrigeration rooms.

In addition to the pumps that dispersed the water supply to the camp, the pump house also contained a central heating system consisting of two fuel oil boilers that provided heat not only for the pump house but for the other buildings used throughout the winter at Camp Ripley.

In order to dispose of Camp Ripley's garbage, a one-ton-capacity, wood-burning incinerator was constructed in the camp's utility area in 1941. In addition to garbage and paper, the incinerator also was equipped to handle tin cans. To this end, the incinerator building housed soaking tanks and can washers. An additional five-ton, wood-burning incinerator was added later, bringing the capacity of the facility to six tons.

A gasoline refueling island was built in 1940 in the camp utility area. Four 13,000-gallon tanks stored the gasoline.

For storage of small arms, one magazine was built in the first phase of construction. An example is shown in this photograph. Three more were built in 1934, and they were located in the utility area.

Housed in this building was a diesel generator that supplied power in case of power failure. Electrical transformers were also located in this structure. It was built in 1943 in the camp utility area.

40

Camp Ripley had its own firefighting system. There was a hook and ladder truck complete with hoses, pumps, and chemical fire retardants intended for use in fighting structural fires. A second truck, outfitted with shovels, portable tanks, and pumps was intended for use in fighting grass and forest fires. The Camp Ripley fire truck has been restored and is in the possession of the Minnesota Military Museum.

This photograph shows the sewage treatment plant in the early phases of its construction. It was designed so that it could be easily expanded to handle greater capacity in the future as Camp Ripley grew.

The gun shed was built in 1930. It was used for storage and repair of small arms. In later years, the ordnance shop performed weapons repair.

This photograph is of the Camp Ripley Ordnance Shop. The project was part of a $360,000 building program at Camp Ripley that had been approved by the Department of War in 1947. Plans to build the shop were announced in June of that year by Brig. Gen. Joseph E. Nelson, who was Minnesota's assistant adjutant general at the time. Once the shop was completed, the intent was that Camp Ripley would serve as the headquarters for repairs of all Minnesota National Guard vehicles, artillery, small arms, and signal equipment. Construction was completed in 1949. In later years, this facility would become known as the Combined Support Maintenance Shop or CSMS.

Three

HISTORICALLY SIGNIFICANT SITES AND BUILDINGS

The construction of the Camp Ripley Post Headquarters was completed in November 1930 at a total cost of $12,461.30. It addition to offices, it contained an officers' lounge, mess hall, and kitchen that would accommodate about 50 officers. Officer's billets, or sleeping quarters, were located on the second floor. This building would later become known as Nelson Hall. It was named after former adjutant general Maj. Gen. Joseph E. Nelson.

In the post headquarters, the officers had their own dining room and a staff that cooked and served their homemade meals. Two of the cooks, Mary Krause and "Ma" Wagner, are shown here preparing meatballs in the kitchen.

The kitchen staff and dining room staff are pictured in this photograph. These people, as well as the housekeepers, were all local residents employed by Camp Ripley.

The cooks prepared elaborately decorated cakes for special occasions. Here Ma Wagner displays one of her creations.

Here is a view of the officers' lounge area in the post headquarters. The fieldstone fireplace was the center of attraction in this room. The furniture was comfortable and abundant, giving the room an elegant, but comfortable, atmosphere.

The post headquarters building was remodeled and modernized many times during the years following its original construction. During one renovation, solid maple–paneled wainscoting, which had been salvaged from the old Minnesota state capitol building, was added to the interior decor.

A very unique feature on the grounds of Nelson Hall is located on the back side of the building within the paved, circular drive. It is a white stone arrow pointing north. A flagpole was later placed in the center of the arrow shaft. The stone arrow shown in the aerial photograph is seen in the foreground of the photograph below, as is the circular drive. On display inside the circular drive is a battery of three steel-rifled cannons that were a gift to the 1st Minnesota Volunteer Infantry Regiment from Maj. Gen. H. S. Sanford, the U.S. minister at Brussels, Belgium, in April 1862.

The battery of three steel-rifled cannons on display behind Nelson Hall was a gift to the 1st Minnesota Volunteer Infantry Regiment from Maj. Gen. H. S. Sanford, U.S. minister at Brussels, Belgium. Sanford had visited Minnesota and heard details of the regiment's valorous performance at the Civil War battles of Ball's Bluff and Bull Run. He was so impressed by the bravery and obvious patriotism of the regiment that upon his return to Belgium, he arranged for these three cannons to be shipped to the United States and presented to the regiment as an expression of his appreciation of their discipline and efficiency. Two National Guardsmen, dressed in attire typical of the 1st Minnesota Volunteer Infantry during the early part of the Civil War, pose for a close-up shot of one of these historic cannons. More clearly illustrated in the photograph below, the uniforms consisted of a red shirt, black trousers, black hat, and gray blanket roll.

Rossberg Hall, also known as building U-1, was built in 1931. The building is completely fireproof with metal doors throughout the entire structure. Aside from the United States Property and Disbursing Office on the first floor, the engineering office and drafting room on the second floor, and a small kitchen and dining room in the basement, the remaining 60 feet by 200 feet of the building is a warehouse complete with ramps for truck access. There is a truck platform used for loading and unloading on the north side and a loading platform adjacent to the railroad track on the south side of the building. There are bars over the windows in the building. The offices in the building are completely air-conditioned. The building was named for Col. Raymond A. Rossberg, who was the U.S. property and disbursing officer and state quartermaster. He was also the camp commander during non-field-training periods.

The Camp Ripley Armory was built in 1937 by the WPA. The central focal point in this building was the large, open area on the ground floor known as the drill floor. It was used for formations and large meetings. Since the building had a stage, most speakers addressed a crowd from a podium on the stage. However, after a fire damaged the interior of the building, reconstruction work was needed and the stage was eliminated. Prior to 1953, when the new camp theater and visual aids training facility was built, the armory served as the main post theater.

The building in this photograph is the office of the Camp Ripley construction quartermaster Maj. Philip C. Bettenburg. He and his engineering firm in St. Paul were responsible for the design of most of Camp Ripley's early buildings and infrastructure. Because the federal government was underwriting most of the cost of construction, all plans had to be approved by architects employed by the federal government.

Valhalla, the governor's lodge, was built in 1934 and 1935 with funds provided by FERA and the State of Minnesota. The total cost of the building was $13,852. Even though it later became the governor's cabin, it was originally known as the 34th Infantry Division Headquarters. Valhalla sustained serious damage from a fire due to a lightning strike on a nearby pine tree in 1968. A total of $25,000 was spent in order to restore the cabin to its original condition. In addition to hosting many VIP social events, Valhalla is a showcase of beautiful gifts received by Camp Ripley over the years, most of which are from Norway. The United States and Norwegian reciprocal troop exchange began in 1974, and most of the paintings, wood carvings, glassware, statues, and rosemaling items have been received from Norwegians visiting Camp Ripley on the exchange program.

Normally for the purposes of historical documentation, a garage would not be worth mentioning. However, the three-car garage available for use by guests staying in Valhalla is unique. Built in 1937, it had a fireplace to keep the cars inside warm and ready to start on cold winter mornings. The barbecue shelter (below), located on the grounds of the governor's lodge, is a unique structure as well. Part of the building is the remains of an old frontier homestead dating from 1850 that was previously located on lands acquired by the State of Minnesota for the expansion of Camp Ripley. The hand-pounded copper lanterns with glass inserts on the front of the structure were salvaged from the original Camp Ripley Post Exchange that was built in 1934. The patio floor is paved with slabs of Cold Spring granite.

The post exchange has existed in several different forms on Camp Ripley. In addition to the main post exchange building where soldiers could purchase merchandise and beverages, several satellite or sub-camp exchanges were located throughout the cantonment area, including one in the service club. The first main post exchange building was built in 1934. It had several different counters where merchandise such as souvenirs, clothing, tobacco, and jewelry could be purchased. There was also a snack bar on the premises.

This building is the only surviving civilian structure on Camp Ripley. Now commonly referred to as the old schoolhouse, it actually was the Green Prairie District No. 12 school. It was built in 1930 to provide a replacement school for the original one that was situated on land purchased by the state for Camp Ripley. While it is now located on the grounds of Camp Ripley, when it was built it was outside the south perimeter fence. The building was acquired by the National Guard in 1950 and is presently used as office space.

There were nine farms located on the land purchased by the State of Minnesota for Camp Ripley. This barn is but one example of civilian structures that remained on the land after the families relocated. Eventually, however, all of them were torn down.

This home was owned by the Mahoney family when it was purchased by the State of Minnesota as part of the Camp Ripley land acquisitions.

This farmstead belonged to the Love family before it was purchased by the State of Minnesota. It, too, was eventually torn down.

Three cemeteries and several grave sites were also located on the land purchased for Camp Ripley. However, only one of the cemeteries is in the cantonment area. The plat for Green Prairie Cemetery was originally filed in 1889, but there are some graves within it that actually predate formal establishment of the cemetery.

A granite wall of similar structure to the others on Camp Ripley was built around the perimeter of the cemetery by WPA workers. Two gateposts of mortared fieldstone and an iron gate were also placed at the cemetery entrance. The most distinguishing feature of this cemetery is the black granite crypt of former adjutant general Ellard A. Walsh who died in 1975. Though the above photograph shows the cemetery overgrown and unkempt, it is now beautifully maintained by the Camp Ripley roads and grounds staff, as evidenced by the photograph below.

THE TOWNSHIP OF
GREENE PRAIRIE
WAS SO NAMED TO PERPETUATE IN
GLORIOUS REMEMBRANCE
CHARLES H. GREENE
CORPORAL I COMPANY THIRD MINNESOTA
VOLUNTEER INFANTRY REGIMENT WHO
WITH TWENTY MEN, SEVERAL CONVALESCENTS
AND A FEW COOKS AND TEAMSTERS ON
THE EVENING OF JULY 13TH 1862 RESISTED
TWO SUCCESSIVE CHARGES BY KENTUCKIANS
AND THREE COMPANIES OF GEORGIA TROOPS.
IT WAS NOT UNTIL THE CONFEDERATE GENERAL
FORREST HAD APPEALED TO THE MANHOOD
OF HIS SUPERIOR FORCES AND PERSONALLY
LEAD A THIRD CHARGE THAT THE HANDFUL OF
COURAGEOUS MINNESOTA TROOPS WERE OVER-
COME. IN THIS, THE BATTLE OF MURFREESBORO,
TENNESSEE, CORPORAL GREENE GAVE UP HIS
LIFE FOR HIS COUNTRY. . . . . . .

Col. Raymond A. Rossberg and two guests are viewing the sign that gives information about Cpl. Charles H. Greene, the man whose name was given to Greene Prairie Township. Greene had a homestead in the area before he volunteered for service with Company I, 3rd Minnesota Volunteer Infantry Regiment and went to fight for the Union cause in the Civil War. At the Battle of Murfreesboro on July 13, 1862, Greene and a small group of men resisted two successive charges of Georgia troops. Not until Confederate general Nathan Bedford Forrest himself lead a third charge were the courageous men, including Greene, defeated and killed. This sign was placed on Camp Ripley to memorialize Greene's sacrifices for his country and to document the story behind the naming of Greene Prairie Township.

Four

LARGE-SCALE ARMY MANEUVERS AT CAMP RIPLEY

Expansion of both the regular army and National Guard forces in 1935 prompted planning of the first large-scale army maneuvers held at Pine Camp in New York in August 1935. From that time on, yearly exercises of a similar nature were ordered. In 1936, preliminary plans were made for maneuvers to be held during the summer of 1937 at Camp Ripley and at Fort Riley in Kansas. This photograph shows troops disembarking from trains in August 1937 at Camp Ripley as they arrived for the maneuvers.

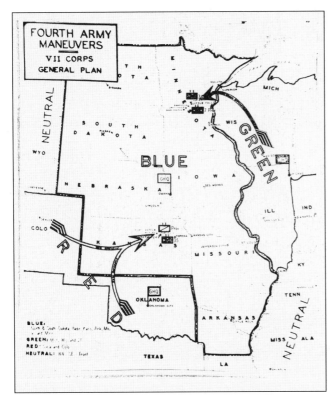

This map shows a rough plan for the 1937 maneuvers. Arrows indicate the locations of Camp Ripley and Fort Riley in Kansas. Some of the situations to be included in the field exercises on August 16–19, 1937, were marching, bivouacs, reconnaissance, and limited night maneuvers.

This photograph was taken at an officer briefing held at the Camp Ripley Armory during the 1937 maneuvers.

A review parade was held on August 15, 1937, at Camp Ripley following unit training that had taken place beginning August 10. August 15 had been designated as Governors Day with the governors of Iowa, North Dakota, South Dakota, and Minnesota attending the parade for review of all the units. Other distinguished guests present that day included Lt. Gen. Friedrich von Boetticher of Germany, Maj. Ivan Okunev of the Soviet Union, Maj. R. G. Whitelaw of Canada, and Brig. Jose Amezcua of Mexico.

This photograph depicts a military band marching in the August 15, 1937, review parade on the grounds of Camp Ripley.

The blue team, which consisted of both regular army and National Guard troops, was camped approximately nine miles north of Swanville. This photograph is an aerial shot of the Swanville Camp. The green team consisted of 34th Infantry Division (National Guard) troops and was based out of Camp Ripley.

Field camps for the 1937 maneuvers consisted of hundreds and hundreds of tents set up in open fields on land that had been leased by the federal government.

This photograph shows two soldiers at one of the field camps washing down a picnic table in the hot summer sun.

The Camp Ripley Armory held the 7th Corps Headquarters for the 1937 maneuvers. The progress of the field exercises was monitored here.

Marching was only one of the many activities on the agenda during the August 1937 maneuvers. This photograph shows troops on a road march.

The men of B Battery, 151st Field Artillery, fire their 75-millimeter howitzers as part of the field exercises.

Once again in 1940, 50,000 regular army and National Guard troops descended on the Camp Ripley area in preparation for large-scale field exercises similar to those held in 1937. The 109th Observation Squadron participated in the 1940 maneuvers as they had in 1937. A total of 55 planes participated in the exercises. The chief task of the aviators was to coordinate between air and ground troops and to assist ground troops in reading aerial photographs. This photograph was taken during the 1940 maneuvers.

On August 12, 1940, the second day of the maneuvers, Gen. George C. Marshall made a special trip to Camp Ripley to inspect all aspects of the field exercises. During his four-hour visit he visited the 7th Corps Headquarters at the armory and reviewed plans for the exercises. He is shown here with Gen. Ellard A. Walsh (right) at the hangar.

Five

HISTORY OF
MILLER AIRFIELD

Minnesota's 109th Observation Squadron was the first National Guard air unit in the country to be federally recognized. The commander, Capt. Ray S. Miller, was also the driving force in organizing the unit. The first field training at Camp Ripley for the squadron took place in the summer of 1931 even though a hangar was not yet constructed. To provide temporary shelter for the airplanes, two hangars were disassembled in West Virginia and reassembled on Camp Ripley. Plans were drawn up by P. C. Bettenburg in June 1931 for the construction of a 66-foot-by-182-foot aircraft hangar. The hangar was built by Northland Construction Company of Minneapolis and completed in 1932.

This aerial photograph of the airfield was taken in 1936. Behind the hangar, to the north, are the tents used to house the aviators as well as the latrines and mess hall. This area was also intended for housing the combat engineer and medical regiments.

This aerial photograph was taken very early in Camp Ripley's development. Note that there is not yet a hangar on the north end of the airfield.

This aerial photograph offers a view of the airfield from the north looking south toward post headquarters.

This photograph was taken in 1939. The double-winged aircraft are Douglas O-38 planes. The single-wing planes are North American O-47 observation planes. Minnesota's 109th Observation Squadron received the first of these new planes in 1938. They were powered by a Cyclone engine with a top speed of 251 miles per hour. The crew consisted of a pilot, radio operator, and gunner.

In August 1930, Minnesota's 109th Observation Squadron received four Douglas O-38 airplanes that, at that time, were the newest aircraft used by the Army Air Corps. They had 525-horsepower Hornet engines. These were the planes flown by the unit during their first training encampment at Camp Ripley in 1932.

These aircraft are North American O-47 observation planes. The picture was taken in 1939.

During the 1940 army maneuvers at Camp Ripley, 14 army P-22 pursuit planes were flown in from Barksdale Field in Louisiana. This aircraft had a cruising speed of 225 to 250 miles per hour.

The critique of the 1937 Fourth Army maneuvers revealed the need for better training of National Guard troops. However, desperately needed additional funding was not forthcoming from the federal government before the following summer. Nonetheless, in June 1938, Minnesota's National Guard infantrymen participated in mock battles. Marine Corps and U.S. Naval Reserve airplanes took part in these exercises. This photograph shows some of the Naval Reserve airplanes.

This photograph shows a U.S. Navy aircraft refueling truck parked outside the Camp Ripley hangar during the 1938 mock battle exercises.

This photograph of the Camp Ripley hangar was taken during the 1940 army maneuvers.

Gen. George C. Marshall, U.S. Army chief of staff, paid a special visit to Camp Ripley during the Fourth Army maneuvers in August 1940. He is shown here at the airfield with Adj. Gen. Ellard A. Walsh on the far right.

During the 1940 Fourth Army maneuvers, another distinguished guest was Minnesota governor Harold Stassen, who was flown to Camp Ripley in an O-47. He is shown here with Adj. Gen. Ellard A. Walsh and with Maj. Ray S. Miller.

Six

LIFE FOR THE TROOPS

Most troops arriving for annual training encampments did so by train. as shown in this 1949 photograph. The trains entered Camp Ripley through the east gate, and the men exited the cars on the south side of Rossberg Hall.

While not in the field, during annual summer training encampments troops lived in canvas tents with wooden frames. The floors of the tents were raised concrete platforms. The photograph below, taken looking north down what is now known as "kitchen road," shows enlisted men's mess halls on the left.

Every fall, tent canvas was removed and stored indoors in an effort to preserve it. However, in the 1950s it became evident that the tents were too expensive and difficult to maintain. Moving toward the intent of making Camp Ripley viable for use during the entire year, the tents were replaced with metal buildings called hutments. In the officers' housing area, two men occupied one hutment. In the enlisted men's area, two sets of double bunks were placed in each hutment, allowing for accommodation of four men.

As depicted in this photograph, guard detail was a reality of life during annual training. Troops pulled guard duty day and night in all types of weather.

One of the more pleasant parts of annual training was getting paid. Prior to leaving for home, the men would have to wait their turn in line to receive their pay in cash, as depicted in this photograph. The men in the above photograph are from the 125th Field Artillery.

While not in the field, chow was cooked and served at the mess hall. This photograph shows men standing in line to wash their mess kits and utensils in a garbage can of hot, soapy water.

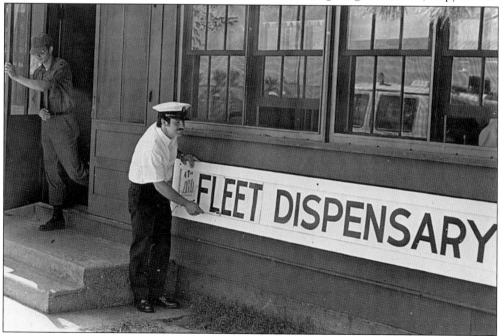

Occasionally the dispensary, or hospital, was manned by people other than army medical personnel. This photograph shows the U.S. Navy was getting ready to take a turn providing medical services to the troops training on Camp Ripley.

Sometimes just relaxing in the tent after a long, hot day was a welcome respite from the rigors of training. Writing letters, playing cards, and reading were common activities on hot summer evenings.

During their off-duty hours, soldiers could patronize the post exchange at any of its several locations around Camp Ripley to buy merchandise or beverages.

This photograph is of a regimental band on the march in the early days of Camp Ripley.

Occasionally soldiers at Camp Ripley received entertainment from outside sources. In this photograph, as part of their mission the 294th army band from North Dakota serenades the troops in 1951.

Sometimes the men brought their own musical instruments from home when they came to Camp Ripley. They got together with other musicians and entertained their fellow soldiers during evenings and off-duty hours.

During the evenings and times when they were off duty, the soldiers found creative ways to pass the time and have a little fun. This photograph, taken in 1936, depicts one unit's amusing form of entertainment—chariot races. The chariots were ammunition handcarts.

Directly south of the infantry a regimental area was the combination hostess house and enlisted men's club. This facility also housed a sub-camp post exchange and the visitors' infirmary. It was complete with a jukebox, piano for sing-alongs, tables, and various games for the enjoyment of the men. The hostess house was later known as the service club. It was constructed in 1934 with funds provided by FERA and had a capacity of 200 people.

This early photograph of the hostess house shows a view of the south side of the building. Note the railroad tracks in the foreground.

While some men wrote letters in their tents in their spare time, others chose to go to the service club to do so.

This soldier from Company D, 136th Infantry, is taking some time to write to a special someone back home during annual training in 1954.

There certainly was no lack of enjoyable activities at the service club.

These men are relaxing by playing cards and reading the newspaper in front of the jukebox at the service club.

For those who did not make their own music but enjoyed hearing it, in addition to the impromptu concerts by their fellow soldiers, they could also go to the service club to listen to music. The club came equipped with a jukebox and a record player. The photograph was taken in 1949.

Quite a crowd has gathered around these checker players at the service club in 1949.

Card playing was a popular pastime with military men during the 1950s. While some soldiers played cards in their tents, others came to the service club to play. These young men are playing cribbage. This photograph was taken in 1954.

Two soldiers collide while jumping to return a shot during a volleyball game in the recreational area at Camp Ripley.

The Camp Ripley Theater was built in 1952. Movies provided by the army motion picture service were shown every night during training encampments. The movies shown were feature films, and the films shown there often had not yet been released to the public. Seating capacity was 2,000. The theater was actually a multi-purpose facility since it was also utilized as a visual aids training site.

The first main post exchange building was built in 1934. It had several different counters where merchandise such as souvenirs, clothing, tobacco, and jewelry could be purchased. In addition to the main post exchange building where soldiers could purchase merchandise and beverages, several satellite exchanges were located throughout the cantonment area, including one in the service club.

With an eye toward maintaining good troop morale, a recreational area was built between regimental areas one and two. The above boxing ring was built in 1948, and boxing matches were a regular occurrence through the 1950s. It is obvious, judging by the crowd gathered around the boxing ring in the photograph below, that this was a popular event with the troops.

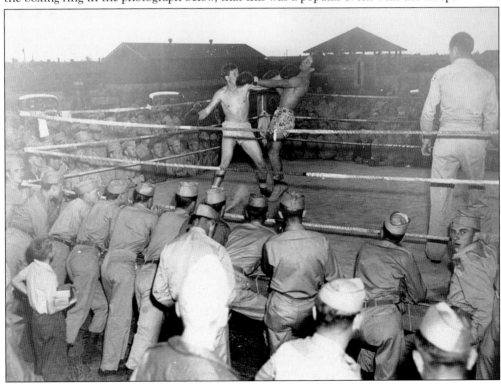

Recreation was a very important part of summer training at Camp Ripley. Evenings and off-duty hours were filled with many enjoyable activities. The post recreational area between areas one and two included baseball and kitten ball diamonds, and games between unit teams were a regular occurrence. In the 1954 photograph above, one of the teams is from Company D, 135th Infantry of Hastings. In the 1951 photograph below, one of the teams is from the 598th Antiaircraft Artillery unit of Duluth.

Troops lined the highway bridge over the Mississippi River to cheer on canoeists competing in a race as part of the Minneapolis Aquatennial celebration during the summer of 1949.

During the 1950s, the Viking Olympics were held during summer annual training encampments at Camp Ripley.

Seven

TRAINING AT CAMP RIPLEY

While on bivouac out in the field, the men lived in two-man tents pitched directly on the ground, as shown in this photograph taken during annual training with the 206th Infantry Regiment in 1935. Prior to proceeding to the field for bivouac, inspections of field equipment were conducted. The inset photograph, taken in 1936, shows an example of how the equipment was displayed on a bunk for such an inspection. A second inspection was completed upon return from the field to check for missing or lost equipment.

On July 1, 1940, the 205th Infantry Regiment was converted into a part of the 215th Coast Artillery Regiment. Prior to the scheduled large-scale army maneuvers the following month, the unit trained for three weeks to familiarize themselves with their new mission and equipment, namely the 90-millimeter antiaircraft gun. Also among the unit's new equipment were 50-inch searchlights. A sister infantry unit was also converted to perform the same mission and redesignated as the 216th Coast Artillery Regiment.

While units were training in the field, the mess section served chow wherever they were located. This photograph shows the chow line for troops of the 47th Infantry Division during the summer of 1949.

Since Camp Ripley is located on the Mississippi River, it offers an ideal opportunity for combat engineer units to practice construction of temporary bridges. This photograph of an M-38A1 jeep crossing the bridge was taken in 1958.

During times when range firing was taking place, guards were always posted at the range control point to prevent any unknown or unauthorized traffic and personnel in or near firing ranges and impact areas.

In this photograph, two soldiers from the 136th Infantry Regiment are working with the 3.5-inch rocket launcher while on annual training at Camp Ripley during the summer of 1958.

An artillery crew is firing a Howitzer during 1958 annual training at Camp Ripley.

During artillery firing, the sounds of exploding rounds could be heard over a wide area surrounding Camp Ripley each summer. These men of Battery B, 1st Battalion, 175 Field Artillery, are firing an eight-inch Howitzer.

Three men from the 1st Battalion, 194th Armory Unit are unpacking tank rounds from wooden ammunition crates and preparing them for use. This photograph was taken in 1958.

Two tank crews take a break out in the field in 1955. The tank in the background of the photograph is an M4 Sherman.

This photograph depicts platoon rifle inspection during annual training in 1958 for troops of the 135th Infantry Regiment, 47th Infantry Division.

These men are firing the Browning Automatic Rifle, also known as the BAR, on the range. It was a very effective weapon that was used from early World War II through the Vietnam War.

Two men from 136th Infantry Regiment, 47th Infantry Division, are practicing sighting and aiming a 57-millimeter recoilless rifle during annual training in June 1958. This particular model of recoilless rifle was a crew-served weapon used during World War II and the Korean War.

In addition to using them as ground weapons on a tripod, recoilless rifles were also mounted on jeeps. In this photograph, a 90-millimeter recoilless rifle is mounted on a specially designed model of jeep called the M38A1C.

Communication is an extremely important aspect of field training. Two men from the 151st Field Artillery Regiment of the 47th Infantry Division are working with the radio during annual training in 1949 at Camp Ripley.

Men from the 175th Field Artillery Regiment, 47th Infantry Division, are loading carbine clips with .30-caliber ammunition in preparation for firing on the rifle ranges during field training in the summer of 1949 at Camp Ripley.

In July 1949, the 5th Army Air Transportability Demonstration Team performed a 1,000-foot jump for troops of the 47th Infantry Division. Special demonstrations of these types were often watched by the public as well as the troops. This particular jump was also witnessed by guests for the annual Legislators' Day at Camp Ripley.

In this photograph taken in 1955, an amphibious DUKW is being used for transporting troops. DUKWs were used extensively in Minnesota by the National Guard largely during flood disasters when the governor activated the guard to assist in evacuation of flooded areas.

Severe weather is not an uncommon occurrence during summer annual training periods at Camp Ripley. Minnesota's hot, humid summers create ideal conditions for sudden heavy rain, windstorms, hail, and tornadoes. During one hot August evening in the mid-1950s, a severe thunderstorm produced heavy rain and wind, which caused extensive damage to the troop housing areas. In this particular storm, one complete row of officer tents was virtually leveled by strong winds. Troops spent the entire next day cleaning up debris and reconstructing the demolished tents.

These men are at practice firing a .30-caliber machine gun during the summer of 1958. Over 7,000 troops were attending annual training at that time.

The "Honest John" rocket was a large-caliber field rocket. It was powered by a solid fuel engine. The rockets were shipped to firing sites in three parts and could be assembled and mounted on the launcher (that was part of a specially modified heavy truck) by six men and a crane in five minutes. There were units of the Minnesota National Guard trained to fire these rockets, and this photograph was taken of a rocket fired at Camp Ripley. During the 1950s, the firing of an "Honest John" rocket signaled the end of many parades.

These men of the 194th Tank Battalion were on a five-mile hike during the summer of 1947. This was the first year that the National Guard had participated in annual training at Camp Ripley since 1940.

Several concrete combat pits were constructed on Camp Ripley.

These men are testing a field switchboard that they have just set up during annual training in 1958. Note the wiring diagram on the display for reference in the background.

This photograph, taken in 1936, is of a unit of the 151st Field Artillery Regiment preparing to move some of its towed Howitzer artillery guns.

After World War I, when the army was searching for a light, high-speed vehicle to move troops, several companies built prototypes for testing. This particular model is one made by Minneapolis-Moline Power Implement Company, and these prototypes were tested at Camp Ripley.

This photograph shows how telephone line is laid in a winter combat situation. The men are on skis, and the cart used for hauling the wire spool is also modified so it is on skis.

Two men are taking a look at a sign erected at the site of old Fort Ripley by the Mississippi River. Signs are currently in place marking the location of each of the original buildings.

As part of its field training, an engineering unit has created a raft that is being used to move an M-38A1 jeep across the river.

In yet another field training exercise, an engineering unit has created a bridge across the river to be utilized for troop crossings.

These two men have assumed an observation position out in the field, with rifles ready, while one communicates via radio.

These men are practicing aiming and firing a 3.5-inch rocket launcher at several targets, including a tank.

Proper use of a gas mask is essential when making a required trip through a tear gas chamber. Tear gas was used for the training purposes only.

These men are taking a break out in the field during annual training in 1955.

The same men are taking a field training class. Soldiers refer to these classes as "common task training."

Eight

SPECIAL VISITORS AND EVENTS

During a retreat parade in 1958, Gov. Orville Freeman salutes from the reviewing stand as troops pass by. The third man from the left is Gen. Ellard A. Walsh, and the fourth man is Maj. Gen. Joseph E. Nelson. Pictured at the same parade, this inset photograph is a close-up of Walsh, Freeman, and Nelson.

The 47th Infantry Division band, like any other unit, needs marching practice. This photograph was taken in 1958.

Here the band poses for a photograph on the highway outside the east gate of Camp Ripley. Note the railroad tracks passing on the far right side of the photograph.

The color guard is dressed in replica Civil War uniforms during a parade in 1958.

Band members are not the only ones who need marching practice prior to a parade or regimental review. The troops do also.

Here the color guard poses in 1949 for this picture, which was used to make a real-photo postcard.

In the 1950s, during the middle weekend of a two-week annual training period, parades were held that were open to the public. Troops marched on foot, rode in military vehicles, and passed overhead in helicopters and planes. These young boys, toy rifles at the ready, are observing a parade in 1959.

Upon the of the return of the 47th Infantry Division to Minnesota in 1953 after several years of active duty during the Korean War, a special ceremony was held for the U.S. Army to officially return the division colors.

Minnesota's governors have been regular visitors to Camp Ripley over the years. In this photograph taken in 1936, Gov. Harold Stassen was paying a visit. He and Gen. Ellard A. Walsh (far right) are in the right foreground of this picture.

Honored guests, such as Gov. C. Elmer Anderson, were transported in true military fashion around Camp Ripley. As shown in this 1958 photograph, the transport of choice is an M-38A1 jeep.

Here Gov. Orville Freeman receives the same VIP treatment.

During his 1951 Governor's Day visit to Camp Ripley, Anderson goes through the chow line and shares a meal with the troops at the mess hall.

This photograph shows Anderson reviewing the troops during his 1951 visit while the 47th Infantry Division band plays in the background.

Here Gov. Luther Youngdahl pays a visit to Camp Ripley to participate in an awards ceremony.

Wearing his life jacket, Gov. Elmer Anderson tries out a footbridge constructed by the engineers.

During the summer of 1954, Camp Ripley received a special visit from Franklin Orth, the special assistant secretary for reserve forces under the secretary of the army. This photograph shows him reviewing the troops.

During the 1950s, Governor's Day was held each summer. In this 1954 photograph, several civilians get a close look at a Sherman tank that is on special display for the occasion.

During Legislators' Day in 1957, several legislators venture across a bridge erected by the combat engineers on the Mississippi River in a 2.5-ton truck.

Several veterans of the 135th Infantry Regiment are invited for a special visit to Camp Ripley in 1958. Here they pose for a picture with Gen. Ellard A. Walsh (fifth from left) and Maj. Gen. Joseph E. Nelson (seventh from left).

Shortly after his transatlantic flight, Charles Lindbergh flew his plane, the *Spirit of St. Louis*, back to Little Falls for a visit to his boyhood home. He landed the plane in a field near the town of Fort Ripley (north of the future Camp Ripley) while approximately 2,000 people looked on. Two National Guardsman watched over Lindbergh's plane while he went by car to Little Falls.

Lindbergh (second from right) made a visit to Camp Ripley again in 1939 during annual summer training. Here he is pictured with the commander of the 109th Observation Squadron, Capt. Ray S. Miller (far right).

While visiting with the men of the 109th Observation Squadron, Charles Lindbergh thoroughly checked out their aircraft.

In this photograph, Lindbergh appears to be strapped into the cockpit and ready to fly.

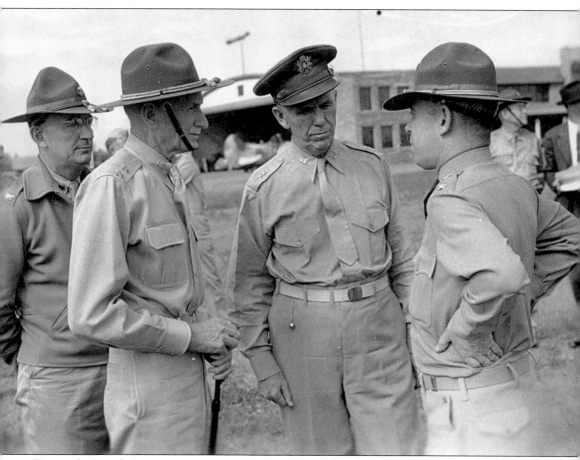

During the Fourth Army maneuvers in 1940, Gen. George C. Marshall paid a visit to Camp Ripley. Here Marshall (center), Maj. Gen. P. P. Bishop, 7th Corps commander (left), and Gen. Ellard A. Walsh discuss plans for troop training.

Former president Harry S. Truman came to Camp Ripley in the summer of 1953. He made a special trip to visit troops from the Missouri National Guard who were training at Camp Ripley. During his visit, he stayed at Valhalla, the governor's lodge. His signature is shown in the guest book there.

In this photograph, Truman is surrounded by a camera-wielding crowd in front of the post headquarters. Maj. Gen. Joseph E. Nelson is in the right foreground.

On the same visit, Truman spoke to a large group at Camp Ripley's post headquarters.

ACROSS AMERICA, PEOPLE ARE DISCOVERING SOMETHING WONDERFUL. THEIR HERITAGE.

Arcadia Publishing is the leading local history publisher in the United States. With more than 3,000 titles in print and hundreds of new titles released every year, Arcadia has extensive specialized experience chronicling the history of communities and celebrating America's hidden stories, bringing to life the people, places, and events from the past. To discover the history of other communities across the nation, please visit:

www.arcadiapublishing.com

Customized search tools allow you to find regional history books about the town where you grew up, the cities where your friends and family live, the town where your parents met, or even that retirement spot you've been dreaming about.

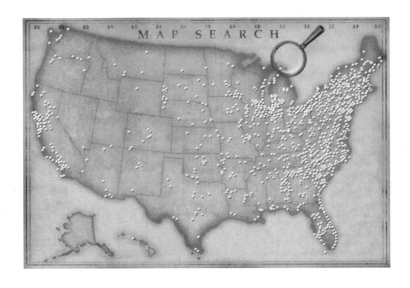